TRIANGLE HISTORIES
★ ★ ★ ★ ★ ★ ★ ★
THE REVOLUTIONARY WAR

# KING
# GEORGE
# III

## Scott Ingram

**BLACKBIRCH®**
**PRESS**

**THOMSON**
—✳—™
**GALE**

San Diego • Detroit • New York • San Francisco • Cleveland
New Haven, Conn. • Waterville, Maine • London • Munich

**LIBRARY OF CONGRESS CATALOGING-IN-PUBLICATION DATA**

Ingram, Scott (William Scott)
  King George III / by Scott Ingram.
    p. cm. — (Triangle history of the American Revolution. Revolutionary War leaders)
Summary: Discusses the early life of King George III, his education,
early turmoil, and the American Revolution as well as his last years and
his role in history.
Includes bibliographical references and index.
  ISBN 1-56711-779-1 (alk. paper)
  1. George III, King of Great Britain, 1738-1820—Juvenile literature. 2. Great Britain—
History—George III, 1760-1820—Juvenile literature. 3. Great Britain—Kings and rulers—
Biography—Juvenile literature. 4. United States—History—Revolution, 1775-1783—
Juvenile literature. [1. George III, King of Great Britain, 1738-1820. 2. Kings, queens,
rulers, etc. 3. Great Britain—History—George III, 1760-1820. 4. United States—History—
Revolution, 1775-1783.] I. Title. II. Series.

  DA506.A2I54 2004
  941'.073'092—dc21

                                                              2003002622

# CONTENTS

# PREFACE: THE AMERICAN REVOLUTION

Today, more than two centuries after the final shots were fired, the American Revolution remains an inspiring story not only to Americans, but also to people around the world. For many citizens, the well-known battles that occurred between 1775 and 1781—such as Lexington, Trenton, Yorktown, and others—represent the essence of the Revolution. In truth, however, the formation of the United States involved much more than the battles of the Revolutionary War. The creation of our nation occurred over several decades, beginning in 1763, at the end of the French and Indian War, and continuing until 1790, when the last of the original thirteen colonies ratified the Constitution.

More than two hundred years later, it may be difficult to fully appreciate the courage and determination of the people who fought for, and founded, our nation. The decision to declare independence was not made easily—and it was not unanimous. Breaking away from England—the ancestral land of most colonists—was a bold and difficult move. In addition to the emotional hardship of revolt, colonists faced the greatest military and economic power in the world at the time.

The first step on the path to the Revolution was essentially a dispute over money. By 1763, England's treasury had been drained in order to pay for the French and Indian War. British lawmakers, as well as England's new ruler, King George III, felt that the colonies should help to pay for the war's expense and for the cost of housing the British troops who remained in the colonies. Thus began a series of oppressive British tax acts and other laws that angered the colonists and eventually provoked full-scale violence.

King George III

   The Stamp Act of 1765 was followed by the Townshend
Acts in 1767. Gradually, colonists were forced to pay
taxes on dozens of everyday goods from playing cards to
paint to tea. At the same time, the colonists had no say in
the passage of these acts. The more colonists complained
that "taxation without representation is tyranny," the
more British lawmakers claimed the right to make laws

for the colonists "in all cases whatsoever." Soldiers and tax collectors were sent to the colonies to enforce the new laws. In addition, the colonists were forbidden to trade with any country but England.

Each act of Parliament pushed the colonies closer to unifying in opposition to English laws. Boycotts of British goods inspired protests and violence against tax collectors. Merchants who continued to trade with the Crown risked attacks by their colonial neighbors. The rising violence soon led to riots against British troops stationed in the colonies and the organized destruction of British goods. Tossing tea into Boston Harbor was just one destructive act. That event, the Boston Tea Party, led England to pass the so-called Intolerable Acts of 1774. The port of Boston was closed, more British troops were sent to the colonies, and many more legal rights for colonists were suspended.

Finally, there was no turning back. Early on an April morning in 1775, at Lexington Green in Massachusetts, the first shots of the American Revolution were fired. Even after the first battle, the idea of a war against England seemed unimaginable to all but a few radicals. Many colonists held out hope that a compromise could be reached. Except for the Battle of Bunker Hill and some minor battles at sea, the war ceased for much of 1775. During this time, delegates to the Continental Congress struggled to reach a consensus about the next step.

During those uncertain months, the Revolution was fought, not on a military battlefield, but on the battlefield of public opinion. Ardent rebels—especially Samuel Adams and Thomas Paine—worked tirelessly to keep the spirit of revolution alive. They stoked the fires of revolt by writing letters and pamphlets, speaking at public gatherings, organizing boycotts, and devising other forms of protest. It was their brave efforts that kept others focused on liberty and freedom until July 4, 1776. On that day, Thomas Jefferson's Declaration of Independence left no doubt about the intentions of the colonies. As John Adams wrote afterward, the "revolution began in hearts and minds not on the battlefield."

As unifying as Jefferson's words were, the United States did not become a nation the moment the Declaration of Independence claimed the right of all people to "life, liberty, and the pursuit of happiness." Before, during, and after the war, Americans who spoke of their "country" still generally meant whatever colony was their home. Some colonies even had their own navies during the war, and a few sent their own representatives to Europe to seek aid for their colony alone while delegates from the Continental Congress were doing the same job for the whole United States. Real national unity did not begin to take hold until the inauguration of George Washington in 1789, and did not fully bloom until the dawn of the nineteenth century.

The story of the American Revolution has been told for more than two centuries and may well be told for centuries to come. It is a tribute to the men and women who came together during this unique era that, to this day, people the world over find inspiration in the story of the Revolution. In the words of the Declaration of Independence, these great Americans risked "their lives, their fortunes, and their sacred honor" for freedom.

The Minuteman statue stands in Concord, Massachusetts.

# Introduction:
## "Open and Avowed Rebellion"

The summer of 1775 was a time of great uncertainty for the American colonies. Violent clashes had occurred between colonists and British troops, but war had not been officially declared between Great Britain and America. The newly formed Patriot army under General George Washington was assembled in Cambridge, Massachusetts. Across the Charles River, a large force of British troops fortified Boston. Meanwhile, in Philadelphia, Pennsylvania, the Continental Congress, with delegates from twelve of the thirteen colonies, met to determine a course of action. In London, the British legislative body, Parliament, debated ways to bring the colonies back under control.

The central figure in the conflict between Great Britain and its colonies was King George III, who felt that the trouble in the empire's American colonies was a problem that had gone on too long. Like Parliament, King George wanted the colonies brought under control.

The armed conflict had resulted from years of bitter disagreement over how the colonies should be ruled. In particular, the colonists objected to paying taxes imposed by Great Britain's Parliament. The disagreement led to the blockade of Boston by British troops in 1774 and, finally, to violence in

8

When King George pushed for enforcement of British control of the colonies, patriot troops clashed with British soldiers in a series of battles.

the spring of 1775. On April 19 at Lexington, west of Boston, a force of British troops defeated colonial volunteers known as minutemen—civilians who took their name from a claim that they could be ready to fight at a moment's notice. The red-coated British soldiers continued to nearby Concord, where they in turn suffered a defeat at the hands of the minutemen, who forced them back to Boston.

Despite the fact the colonial troops had fought several battles, there was no clear agreement in the Continental Congress that a complete break from Great Britain was necessary. Many delegates from New England, where the fighting had taken place, were convinced that immediate independence was the only course of action. Delegates from colonies farther south were not convinced that this step was necessary. There had been no clashes in those colonies, and many of the delegates hoped that a compromise could be reached that would give the colonies a greater voice in their government while they remained a part of the British Empire.

As if to emphasize the lack of agreement, the Continental Congress in Philadelphia approved two different documents at almost the same time. One was an offer to Great Britain of terms for a peaceful resolution of the disputes. The other explained to the world at large the reason for the colonists' taking up arms.

On July 5, Congress issued a document known as the Olive Branch Petition—the olive branch was a commonly understood symbol of peace. The document asked the king to stop the taxation policies of the British Parliament and allow colonists a voice in their own government. In return, the members of Congress offered peace and harmony as loyal subjects of the Crown with these words: "The apprehensions which now oppress our hearts with unspeakable grief, being once removed, your Majesty will find your faithful subjects on this

The Continental Congress gathered in Philadelphia to draft statements addressing British control of the colonies.

continent ready and willing at all times . . . to assert and maintain the rights and interests of your Majesty and of our Mother Country."

The next day, July 6, Congress approved a document that was quite different from the Olive Branch Petition. That document, titled the Declaration of the Causes and Necessity of Taking Up Arms, did not declare war. Instead, it explained to fellow colonists and to the world at large the reasons for the decision to fight the British and mainly said that the conflict was over tax policies of the British government. It was written in fiery language that differed from the petition issued a day earlier. The document's conclusion stated: "In our own native land, in defence of the freedom that is our birthright . . . we have taken up arms. We shall lay them down when hostilities shall cease."

When the Olive Branch Petition arrived in London, George III refused to even read it. In late August, the king issued a declaration of his own. In this royal proclamation, he claimed that the colonists were being led onto a treacherous path by "dangerous and ill designing men"—that is, the Continental Congress. The actions of the Congress, whom the king called "traitors," had led to what he termed "open and avowed rebellion."

As far as George Ill was concerned, there would be no olive branches until the rebels were crushed. The royal proclamation left no doubt among the Americans or the British: The American Revolution had begun.

# Chapter 1

For much of the latter half of the eighteenth century, the actions of the British Parliament infuriated most American colonists. The economy of Great Britain was in debt due to wars in Europe and America, and Parliament had decided to solve the problem by forcing the colonies to pay higher taxes. British lawmakers passed tax acts and other laws that affected daily life in the colonies. Even more galling to the colonists was the fact that they were not consulted before these laws were passed.

Because Parliament held sessions in London, most members of that body were unknown to the colonists. The anger of colonists was directed largely at royal colonial governors who were responsible for enforcing Parliament's laws. Colonists also spoke out against the leader of Parliament, known as the prime minister.

OPPOSITE: George III ascended the British throne when he was twenty-two years old. Influenced by Parliament and royal advisers, the young king had less control over the British Empire than colonists thought.

13

There was one individual above all others, however, who was the focus of the colonists' displeasure: King George III. In many ways, George III represented everything that Americans disliked about British rule. He cared nothing for their opinions and believed that colonies were established to serve the greater good of the British Empire. He remained a cold, distant monarch in a land across the Atlantic.

As an individual, however, George III was less than the powerful figure he appeared. Under British law, Parliament had power over the monetary affairs of the king, and it was not required to submit to his demands. The king's appointments to various positions had to be approved in Parliament, and George III was often at odds with the antiroyal members of Parliament.

★

In 1700, the estimated population of the American colonies was 275,000 people.

★

The power of George III was also undermined by unscrupulous family members and scheming advisers. As a result, many of the decisions for which colonists criticized the king were actually made by Parliament and royal advisers. Although colonists thought of him as someone whose absolute rule must be opposed, his reign of almost sixty years was actually one of self-doubt, defeat, and illness.

## Control of British Royalty

The control Parliament wielded over Britain's affairs had its roots in laws that British legislators themselves had passed at the beginning of the eighteenth century. In 1701, Parliament had passed the Act of Settlement, by which Parliament assumed the right to name the heirs in line for the throne.

The Act of Settlement also gave Parliament the power to approve a yearly allowance for the royal family and the right to pass other laws regarding military and economic matters. For example, the act also stated that no wars could be fought without Parliament's approval. Deciding how to pay for fighting wars was also something Parliament took upon itself. The Navigation Acts, a system of taxation that applied to trade between Great Britain and its colonies, were one way Parliament sought to raise money for military expenses.

> ★
> In 1722, Samuel Adams was born in Boston, Massachusetts.
> ★

Although Parliament had given itself the right to name the heirs to the British throne, it had placed one significant limitation on itself: The heirs had to be Protestant. As it happened, the family with the strongest claim to the throne, and which fulfilled the Act of Settlement's requirement that the monarch be Protestant, was actually German. This noble family, the House of Hanover, became Britain's royal family. As a consequence, upon the death of Britain's Queen Anne in 1714, a Hanover became Britain's King George I.

## "Lethargic" and "Incapable"

It was into this new ruling family and its somewhat tense and certain relationship between king and Parliament that the child who would one day rule as King George III was born, on June 4, 1738.

15

# The Navigation Acts

In order to fulfill its responsibilities for the British economy, Parliament had to look for ways to support an expanding empire. In 1696, this responsibility led lawmakers to pass the Navigation Acts. The legislation was intended to raise funds to support the monarchy and to establish economic control over its colonies.

The Navigation Acts required all goods that traveled between British colonies and Great Britain to be carried in English-built ships. In addition, all European goods bound for the colonies had to come from Great Britain or pass through Great Britain to be taxed. Finally, colonial products could be exported only to Great Britain or another British colony.

For the first decades of the acts, the British were involved in European conflicts and did not fully enforce the Navigation Acts. Wealthy colonial merchants were able to avoid the taxes by smuggling goods and, if that failed, paying bribes to tax officers. As a result, any funds that were raised by taxes came from craftsmen and others who could not afford smuggled goods and the cost of bribes. Much of the initial resentment of British tax policies arose in this class of colonists and was focused on the Navigation Acts.

George III was the second of seven children—and the first son—born to Crown Prince Frederick and his wife, Princess Augusta. Although Prince Frederick's father, George II, was Great Britain's king and had held the throne for about ten years, Prince Frederick's son was the first member of the royal family to be born in Great Britain. In fact, neither George II nor Prince Frederick grew up speaking English. Frederick had not even moved to London from the German state of Hanover until several years before the birth of his son.

George III was the first royal family member to be born on British soil. Both his father and grandfather, King George II (above), came from the German state of Hanover

The family into which George III was born was anything but close-knit. George's father, Frederick, had become the object of both his parents' hatred. This dislike had arisen because as a young adult, Frederick had written a book in which he criticized his father's rule, an act that George II considered a terrible insult even coming as it did from the crown prince. George II called Frederick "the greatest villain that ever was born." The crown prince's mother, Queen Caroline, agreed, calling him "the greatest beast in the whole world."

Despite the tensions with his own parents, Frederick was a loving father. He encouraged all of his children to appreciate music and science. He hired tutors to teach his sons Latin, French, German, history, mathematics, and religion. When

17

his oldest son had difficulty learning to read and write, Frederick was patient with him.

George eventually learned to read properly, but not until he was eleven, and even then his handwriting remained a childish, blockish print. His tutors found George a difficult pupil and labeled him "lethargic" and "incapable." He was also temperamental and stubborn when criticized.

George's life changed dramatically in 1751, when his father died. Suddenly, at age thirteen, he was the direct heir to the throne of Great Britain. His mother, who was aware of her son's limitations, knew that he could not succeed as a king without some guidance. She called on a former adviser of her husband, John Stuart, the earl of Bute, to prepare George for the throne.

Over the next nine years, Bute taught the young heir how to handle responsibilities that he would have to face. In the process, he became the main influence in George's life. Bute was a firm believer in the power of the monarchy. He taught young George to demand absolute obedience from those he entrusted with running the nation's affairs. Bute also did much to instill in George his own distrust of Parliament, especially of the House of Commons.

## The French and Indian War

The earl of Bute mentored young George.

While George was under the wing of Bute, Great Britain, under George's grandfather,

King George III

became involved in a war that began in the American colonies and eventually reached Europe. The conflict arose because George II granted a group of wealthy investors, called the Ohio Company, two hundred thousand acres along the Ohio River in the early 1750s. He promised another three hundred thousand acres within seven years if the Ohio Company settled the land. About the same time, colonists were beginning to push west over the Allegheny Mountains and into the Ohio River Valley. The wealthy planters and English nobles who owned the Ohio Company sold land to these settlers for high profits.

The problem was that France, a longtime European rival of Great Britain, also claimed ownership of the land in the Ohio River Valley and was unwilling to see it settled by British subjects. In 1753, France sent fifteen hundred soldiers on a mission south from Lake Erie in northern Ohio to force the English out of the area.

★
In the early 1750s, Thomas Paine worked as an apprentice in his father's corset shop in England.
★

In June 1753, Virginia's royal governor, Robert Dinwiddie, who was also a member of the Ohio Company, wrote to the king about the French actions. George II told the governor to send an ambassador to the French in the Ohio River Valley. The governor's representative was to tell the French that Great Britain was the rightful owner of the territory.

As a messenger, Dinwiddie selected George Washington, a young tobacco planter. In November 1753, Washington and six companions set out to

19

deliver the message to the French at Fort Duquesne, their stronghold on the Ohio River. When he arrived, Washington presented Dinwiddie's letter to the French commander. The next day, the French brought back their written reply. They refused to withdraw.

When Dinwiddie was informed of the French refusal, he ordered Washington to take as many volunteers as possible and return to Fort Duquesne and force the French to leave. On April 2, 1755, Washington assembled more than 130 officers and men and started west. On April 20, Washington's scouts spotted a French force along the Monongahela River, about forty miles south of the Ohio River. Washington led his men to where the French were encamped and ordered his force to open fire. In the brief skirmish, ten French soldiers were killed. In addition, one Virginian was killed and three wounded. The conflict that came to be known as the French and Indian War in the colonies and the Seven Years' War in Europe had begun.

The war soon widened as both the French and the British formed alliances with Native American tribes. In addition, the war spread across the Atlantic as Great Britain formed alliances with European powers.

The foray by Washington and his men, which had begun the war, had failed to dislodge the French from Fort Duquesne, but the British persisted. During the autumn of 1758, Brigadier General John Forbes arrived from Great Britain

Battles ensued between the colonists, French, and British as they fought for control of America.

with orders to march west and attack Fort Duquesne. He formed a group of about fifteen hundred British regulars and more than three thousand Virginians and other colonists. Washington was put in command of the colonial troops.

On November 24, the troops arrived at Fort Duquesne to discover that the French, aware of the coming attack, had blown up the fort and retreated north. Forbes quickly had a work crew erect another fort on the ruins of Fort Duquesne. He named it Fort Pitt, in honor of Great Britain's prime minister, William Pitt. The next year, British forces defeated the French in the Battle of Quebec in Canada, and the war in North America began to wind down.

Just over a year after the Battle of Quebec, another event of great consequence took place in Great Britain. In October 1760, George II died. George, son of Frederick, took the throne and became King George III. He had just turned twenty-two years old.

# Chapter 2

## TURMOIL IN
## THE EARLY REIGN

Ving George III took the throne at a time when
Great Britain's war with France in the American
colonies and in Europe was coming to a close. The
new king had hoped to make Lord Bute the prime
minister, but he decided to allow his grandfather's
prime minister, William Pitt, to remain in the position
as a long period of treaty negotiations began.
Those negotiations finally resulted in the Treaty
of Paris, which officially ended the war in 1763.

OPPOSITE: This painting depicts jubilant colonists as they pull down
a statue of George III. Patriots showed their displeasure with the king
in the years leading up to the Revolutionary War.

23

# "The Great Commoner"

★ ★ ★ ★ ★

William Pitt was one of the most admired prime ministers in eighteenth-century Great Britain. A lifelong member of the antiroyal Whig Party, Pitt was known to the British people as "the Great Commoner." In the British government, the prime minister is the head of the political party that controls Parliament. Most legislation and other acts that are passed by Parliament must first have the approval of the prime minister. Pitt's enormous popularity helped him to dominate the political scene during the late 1750s and early 1760s.

Pitt was the son of a member of Parliament and the grandson of a London merchant, Thomas Pitt, who had helped to build British trade relations with India. He entered Parliament in 1735 at the age of twenty-seven after attending Oxford. After he became prime minister in 1757, Pitt worked to send a powerful British fleet to blockade French ports. His war strategies led to victories over the French in India and Canada and on the seas.

As important as the outcome of the war was to him and his realm, George III was equally concerned with another aspect of his rule: finding a queen. This was important because although Parliament had the right to name the heir to the throne, it generally selected the oldest male child of the living monarch. George III, therefore, wanted to marry and produce legitimate heirs in order to

In 1761, Pitt resigned after George III disagreed with his recommendation that the war should be waged until France was completely defeated in Europe, and then expanded with an attack on the French ally, Spain. Without royal approval, Pitt could not get the votes of the Tory Party he needed to implement his strategy. After he resigned, Pitt became an outspoken critic of the government. He called the 1763 Treaty of Paris that ended the war "too lenient."

From 1766 to 1768, Pitt again served as prime minister. His government, however, was unable to agree on a manner of dealing with America. He supported the Americans' arguments against taxation, but not their desire for independence. With his inability to solve the American question, Pitt became depressed and resigned in 1768.

Pitt returned to Parliament, where he continued to speak out against British policy in the colonies. He collapsed during a speech in Parliament in 1778 and died at the age of seventy. In his day, Pitt was widely known for his criticism of British policy against the American colonies and his skills as a wartime leader during the French and Indian War.

continue his family's hold on the throne. Without an heir, other noble families might approach Parliament and present their claim to be named the royal family.

George III's search for a wife was complicated by both political and religious considerations. At that time, royal marriages were usually arranged to create and strengthen alliances between nations.

Queen Charlotte

George III was also required by law to marry a Protestant. Because his family had German roots, he preferred to marry someone of German nobility to solidify ties with the states there. Therefore, in 1761, Bute helped to arrange a marriage between George III and seventeen-year-old Princess Charlotte Sophia, of the German state of Mecklenberg-Strelitz. Charlotte Sophia left her home in August 1761 and boarded the newly built British yacht *Royal Charlotte* to sail across the North Sea to England. The young woman spoke no English, but during the voyage she memorized a few English sentences.

George met his bride-to-be for the first time when she arrived in London in the fall of 1761. He was said to have been somewhat disappointed because he considered the princess rather plain looking. Nevertheless, the two were married in late 1761, and Princess Charlotte Sophia became Queen Charlotte. Eleven months after the wedding, the first of their fifteen children, named George after his father, was born.

In 1762, while he was still adjusting to the demands of being a ruler, a husband, and a father, George III fell ill. For seven months, from January until July, he suffered from a fever, severe stomach pains, rapid heartbeat, numbness, and sleep

26

problems. The cause of these symptoms was a hereditary disease now known as porphyria, although doctors at the time had no knowledge of this disorder.

## Early Difficulties

His mysterious illness was just one of the many challenges George III faced in the early years of his reign. Some of those challenges he brought on himself because of his immaturity and his tendency to consider members of Parliament and other politicians as little more than servants. The king's attitude caused resentment in Parliament, as did the fact that because George III was the first ruler in more than thirty years who spoke English rather than German, Parliament had less control over him than it had enjoyed over George I and George II.

The most critical challenge to the king, the Parliament, and the country was the payment of the national debt, which had more than doubled to 100 million pounds in less than ten years. The future of Great Britain's government and the monarchy were at risk due to the economic problems this debt caused. The only solution to the debt problem, in the view of Parliament, was to increase taxes.

★

In 1765, Thomas Paine, employed as a tax collector for King George III, was fired for incompetence.

★

By this time, William Pitt had been replaced as prime minister by Lord Bute, George III's longtime mentor. Lord Bute made two proposals to help the poor economy, but both made him—and thus the

27

# Porphyria

Porphyria, the modern name for the disease that affected George III throughout his life, was familiar to anyone close to the royal family. It had also incapacitated other family members. Doctors at the time, however, had no idea about the cause of or cure for the peculiar illness. During the first encounter with the disease, George III felt better several times, then relapsed. Unknown to him and his medical advisers, attacks of the disease were brought on by use of alcohol and exposure to the sun.

Porphyria, which was passed down to George III through his mother's family, is caused by the lack of a chemical called hemoglobin in the red blood cells. Its symptoms are sensitivity to light, abdominal pain, rapid heartbeat, and purplish urine. When porphyria affects the skin, blisters, itching, and swelling generally occur. Attacks of the disease increase in severity over time. As the disease progresses, it causes numbness in the arms and legs due to interrupted nerve impulses. The interrupted nerve impulses eventually reach the brain and can cause mental disorders such as depression, anxiety, and paranoia.

Today, porphyria can be controlled by drugs and diet. Medicine in George III's time had not developed to that point. Doctors usually resorted to draining what they considered bad blood from ill patients, a practice called bleeding.

king—highly unpopular. The first of these proposals was to leave in place the yearly land tax, which had been doubled during the war. The second proposal was to tax wine and hard cider in the same way that beer was already taxed. Bute's two proposals enraged most of the British populace.

British citizens protested taxes on wine, hard cider, and land implemented by Lord Bute and George III.

Bute's plan was narrowly approved by Parliament, and right away, public protests broke out across Great Britain. There were riots, and mobs hung dummies or symbols of Bute—most often boots, because of the similarity in sound—in effigy, People threw stones at members of Parliament as they walked in the streets, and the windows in Bute's home in London were smashed.

Bute's plans had considerable opposition in Parliament. One member of the House of Commons, John Wilkes, was particularly outspoken in his criticism of Bute and his influence over the king. In June 1762, Wilkes founded a newspaper and began to publish articles that attacked the prime minister and George III. In his articles, Wilkes charged that the king lacked not only

29

experience but also intelligence. Wilkes also charged that George III, under Bute's influence, had misrepresented the Treaty of Paris when, in a speech, the king had called it "honourable to my Crown and beneficial to my people." Wilkes claimed that the treaty was weak because it did not punish the French enough.

A member of Parliament, John Wilkes founded a newspaper and published articles that attacked George III for his taxes.

Wilkes's attacks continued for nearly a year. Eventually, Bute persuaded the king to have Wilkes arrested and tried on charges of libel—publishing untrue statements—and treason. At Wilkes's trial, however, a judge ruled that Wilkes, as a member of Parliament, was immune from arrest of any sort.

Once freed, Wilkes immediately resumed his published attacks. Finally, a supporter of George III challenged Wilkes to a pistol duel. In the exchange of gunfire, both men were wounded. Because dueling was against the law for members of Parliament, Wilkes was expelled from the House of Commons. This meant that he could be arrested for the previous charges. Before he could be arrested, however, Wilkes fled to France.

The conflict with Wilkes hurt the popularity of George III, and it left Bute with so little support in Parliament that he resigned. Bute's resignation did

30

not mean an end to the taxes he had backed, which in any case were not sufficient to solve the economic problems of Great Britain. George III asked his new prime minister, Lord George Grenville, to look to the American colonies for additional revenue.

## The Stamp Act

George III's choice of Grenville to help solve the nation's financial problems was not popular with many British. The new prime minister not only supported Bute's tax plans, but he had also been among the members of Parliament who had voted to expel and arrest the popular Wilkes. Grenville sought to regain public approval for the king with a new solution to the economic crisis. First he proposed lowering taxes slightly on British subjects at home. He then proposed new taxes only applying to the colonies that would more than replace the revenue—from the lowered domestic taxes.

Grenville's plan was popular with members of Parliament, who saw lowering taxes at home

Lord George Grenville, prime minister to King George III, led the 1765 passage of the Stamp Act.

as an opportunity to boost their own popularity. Lawmakers justified their actions by saying that if colonists wanted to enjoy the protection of the British government, they should pay for that protection. The British public agreed.

As part of his strategy, Grenville gave his support to two additional ways of raising revenue that had been suggested while Bute had been prime minister. In 1764, the Sugar Act and the Currency Act were added to Navigation Acts, which had been in place for more than sixty years. These two new laws required colonists to buy sugar only from British colonies in the West Indies and to pay for what they bought only with British money. The idea behind these laws was to channel money from the colonies to the British treasury.

The problem with these acts was the same as with the original Navigation Acts passed in 1696: enforcement. Rich colonial merchants had commonly smuggled goods in and out of Boston and other colonial ports in the early 1700s. They had gotten away with violation of the law because they had paid bribes to royal lawmakers or appointees to allow goods to pass. In similar fashion the wealthiest colonists were able to obtain and sell non-English sugar simply by paying a bribe. Most colonists had long been infuriated by such corruption. To them, the Sugar and Currency Acts were examples of the way that the British government favored the wealthy.

George III's actions only served to increase the colonists' resentment. Prior to the passage of the new laws, men appointed to tax collection jobs by the king had remained in Great Britain. In general, they had collected their salary and in turn paid colonists to do the actual work for them. It was these colonists who accepted bribes and turned a blind eye to smuggling. After the passage of the Sugar Act and the Currency Act, George III insisted that anyone he appointed to collect taxes had to go to America to do the job. Many colonists lost their positions as a result of this change. In addition, all of the Navigation Acts were now more strictly enforced. The customs officials sent by the king collected every cent they were due and refused to listen to the colonists' objections.

Such a disregard of colonists' concerns was further demonstrated in April 1765, when, under Grenville's leadership, Parliament passed the Stamp Act. Word soon spread from New Hampshire to Georgia that Parliament—and, in their view, George III—expected the colonists to pay the cost of the French and Indian War. Even worse, the Stamp Act also stated that the colonies would have to pay to maintain British troops in America.

Unlike the Navigation Acts, which had mainly applied to merchants, the Stamp Act would affect almost all Americans. The act, which was scheduled to take effect in November 1765, required colonists to buy stamps bearing the royal coat of arms and place them on all papers and legal

Under the Stamp Act, colonists had to affix stamps, like those pictured above, to all paper documents.

documents—wills, deeds, birth certificates, marriage licenses, bills of sale, diplomas, even playing cards and newspapers.

One consequence of the Stamp Act was a weakening of the colonies' ties to Great Britain—just the opposite of what Grenville had intended. Before the Stamp Act, Great Britain had been able to count on the colonists' loyalty, affection, and respect for royal tradition. Most, after all, had come from Great Britain and considered themselves British subjects and therefore supported the king and Parliament.

The Stamp Act, however, outraged colonists. They felt that it was unfair, since they had already paid their share of the war expenses by providing men, money, and supplies. They also pointed out that they already paid local taxes under laws passed by the colonial legislatures. The Stamp Act was, in effect, a double tax. Moreover, it had been passed by a Parliament in which the colonists had no representatives. In the words of Boston colonist James Otis, who spoke out against the Stamp Act in 1765, "Taxation without representation is tyranny."

## Revolt in Boston

In the upheaval over the Stamp Act, one place became a center of protest—the port city of Boston, Massachusetts. Boston was home to a large number of merchants and craftsmen who over the years had built up a strong dislike for British policies connected with the Navigation Acts.

★

In 1765, John Paul Jones, known as John Paul, was a third mate on a British slave ship.

★

Among the Boston residents who led the opposition to the Stamp Act, none was more outspoken than Samuel Adams. Adams had criticized British rule for years. During the summer of 1765, he saw an opportunity to create more widespread resistance to the British. To fan the flames of outrage, he went door to door in Boston and explained how the tax stamps intruded into the life of every colonist.

Adams also sent letters to newspapers and wrote pamphlets in which he protested against the Stamp Act. In his writing, Adams claimed that British taxes on the colonies took away the colonists' freedom. He pointed out that the salaries of colonial officials, who were supposed to oversee the public

35

Angry colonists hung dummies of British officials during the Stamp Acts riots.

good, were paid with funds that came from across the ocean. In other words, the taxes that came from the colonists went into the pockets of royal officials, who did nothing for the colonies in return.

By the summer of 1765, in popular gathering places such as taverns and meetinghouses, discussions grew heated over the Stamp Act. On the night of August 14, 1765, in Boston, colonists met beneath a giant 120-year-old elm, which they called the Liberty Tree. From the tree they hung a dummy in the likeness of Andrew Oliver, the tax stamp distributor. A boot with a devil sticking out of it was suspended by a rope from another branch—a play on the name of the former prime minister who had originally suggested the tax. The message was that the stamp officer and Parliament were in league with the devil. The protests, which carried on for several days, became known as the Stamp Act riots.

The news of the Stamp Act riots eventually reached London. The king, however, was unaware of the colonists' actions because the news arrived at a time when he had suffered another attack of porphyria. This time, the interruptions in nerve impulses affected his brain and led him to suffer what modern medical experts believe was a psychological breakdown. He was alternately deeply depressed, then wildly cheerful, then sulky and agitated in a cycle that went on for weeks in mid-1765.

The illness meant that the king was unable to carry out his normal duties, and this led to awareness in Parliament of the problems the country would face if the king was incapacitated.

Queen Charlotte tends to George III, suffering from a psychological breakdown caused by porphyria, in this still from the film *The Madness of King George*.

Grenville requested a law that would allow the king to name someone to temporarily assume his position during illness. Parliament refused that request and instead formed a Regency Council to carry out royal responsibilities.

The inability of Grenville to carry out the king's wish for regency power led to a break between the two men. Grenville resigned shortly before the Stamp Act was to take effect and was replaced by Charles Watson-Wentworth, marquis of Rockingham.

Meanwhile, as the November 1 date for the Stamp Act to take effect approached, many colonists felt that the time was right to take actions to oppose the law. Adams joined with James Otis to call for a Stamp Act Congress to develop a boycott against the tax. Delegates from nine colonies attended the convention in New York City in October 1765.

When the Stamp Act took effect in November, many colonial merchants and printers ignored it. Boston closed its courts rather than put stamps on official documents. Other cities did the same. With few troops in America, the British Crown could not enforce the tax. The prime minister, who had never favored the tax, pointed out to lawmakers that the cost of sending more troops to America would wipe out any gains from the tax.

Finally in February 1766, Parliament followed Lord Rockingham's request and repealed the Stamp Act. In Boston, colonists celebrated with ringing

# The Sons of Liberty

Among the Boston colonists who were most active in the movement against the Stamp Act besides Samuel Adams were Dr. Joseph Warren and Paul Revere, a silversmith and engraver. In 1764, these Boston colonists formed a group dedicated to opposition of the Stamp Act. In a back room of the Green Dragon Tavern in Boston, they formed the Union Club. That name, however, was soon changed.

Their new name came from a speech by a member of the House of Commons named Isaac Barré, who had spoken out against the passage of the Stamp Act by Parliament. Barré had correctly predicted outrage from the colonists, whom he called "these Sons of Liberty." The name appealed to the new sense of patriotism among many colonists. The Union Club soon changed its name to the Sons of Liberty. Throughout 1764, chapters of the Sons of Liberty formed in New York City, then throughout New England, the Carolinas, and Virginia. The formation of these groups signaled the birth of American political activism.

church bells, fireworks, and parades. Many colonists believed that it was their protests that had forced Grenville from office, and this made the news of the repeal even sweeter. Colonists now applauded King George III, and many believed that good relations could be reestablished with Great Britain.

# Chapter 3

## PROTEST AT HOME
## AND ABROAD

T he effort to repeal the Stamp Act cost the prime
minister, Rockingham, a great deal of political
power in Parliament. Although that body followed
the prime minister's request and repealed the act,
many in Parliament were far from ready to give
up the effort to control the colonies. In return for
voting to repeal the Stamp Act, Rockingham was
forced to put his support behind a declaration that
stated: "Parliament assembled, had, hath and of
right ought to have, full power and authority to
make laws and statutes of sufficient force and
validity to bind the colonies and people of America."

OPPOSITE: Increasing tensions between British soldiers and colonists
led to the Boston Massacre (pictured).

What came to be known as the Declaratory Act reminded the colonists that although Parliament had repealed the Stamp Act, it retained its absolute right to govern "in all cases whatsoever." This, colonists understood, meant that the British government could raise taxes in any way it pleased without colonial representation.

Throughout the conflict over the Stamp Act, George III had been working behind Rockingham's back to select another prime minister. He did so because he realized that the constant change of prime ministers was harming his ability to solve the country's economic problems. The king wanted a prime minister who could build a more stable government and a better relationship with Parliament's House of Commons, where his plans most often encountered opposition.

William Pitt

When Rockingham learned of the king's actions, he resigned. The king then turned back to William Pitt, who had been prime minister when George III had taken the throne. The king felt that Pitt was a good choice because he had long been a member of the House of Commons—in fact, he was known as "the Great Commoner." In addition, Pitt was popular among the American colonists for the way in which he had overseen the conduct of the French and Indian War.

Despite this promise, the king's choice of Pitt proved to be a mistake. At age sixty, Pitt was thirty years older than the king. As he had done when George III first took the throne, Pitt tried to direct the king, which the king deeply resented. In addition, Pitt had become tremendously wealthy in the brief time he had been out of office. Members of the House of Commons no longer considered him an ally, and he was unable to build the strong bond with Parliament that the king had wanted.

Pitt's governing abilities were also impeded by his health. He became ill shortly after taking the post and was forced to turn a great deal of the work he wished to do over to ministers who served under him. One of these individuals was Charles Townshend, the trade minister.

Townshend, who had served in the House of Commons, favored shifting the burden of taxes to the colonies. Less than a year after the passage of the Declaratory Act, Townshend called for a tax on everyday items, such as glass, paint, paper, lead, and tea, as they arrived in American ports. Parliament cooperated and passed these taxes, which were called the Townshend Acts.

Once again, anti-British groups such as the Sons of Liberty and other colonists gathered beneath the Liberty Tree to hang dummies of tax collectors.

Samuel Adams encouraged citizens to boycott British products. Protesters took to the streets again, and vandals broke the windows of merchants who sold British goods.

## Riots in England

At the same time loyalty to the king was wearing thin in the colonies, events at home were putting a strain on George III's relationship with his subjects. When Wilkes returned to England from France in early 1768, he believed that he was still so popular among the people that he would not be arrested. He ran for election to the House of Commons and won by a wide margin.

Although Wilkes had won, Parliament declared the election void because of Wilkes's previous activities. Another election was ordered, and a candidate named by Parliament ran against Wilkes. Again, Wilkes won easily and again Parliament threw out the results. Finally, after four votes, Parliament declared its candidate the winner, even though he had received fewer votes than Wilkes had.

★

In 1768, John Dickinson, author of the Olive Branch Petition, published *Letter from a Farmer in Pennsylvania.*

★

Wilkes immediately resumed his publishing career and wrote several articles in which he insulted both George III and Parliament. The king ordered Wilkes arrested and tried for libel. For weeks, large crowds gathered in a large open area outside of the prison, called St. George's Field, to protest the arrest.

44

Riots in London lasted for weeks as citizens protested the arrest of George Wilkes for libel of the king and Parliament.

In May 1768, a crowd of about fifteen thousand people marched outside the prison and chanted "Wilkes and Liberty," "No Liberty, No King," and "Damn the King! Damn the Government! Damn the Justices!" Fearing that the crowd would attempt to free Wilkes, guards opened fire. Seven people were killed in what came to be known as the Massacre of St. George's Field. The killings were followed by riots across London and weeks of civil unrest. In June, Wilkes was found guilty of libel and sentenced to twenty-two months imprisonment and fined one thousand pounds. The events surrounding Wilkes and Parliament's efforts to

45

exclude him only served to enhance his popularity among ordinary people across Great Britain. The admiration for Wilkes added to George III's many problems in 1768.

Pitt, who had been ill for much of his term, resigned, but not before he called the king and Parliament "incompetent" for their handling of the Wilkes affair. The resignation came at a time when Great Britain was in deep economic distress. The country faced high unemployment and an unusually brutal winter. To make matters worse, it was a year of bad harvests, food shortages, and rising prices.

## Royal Governor's Action

The situation was also growing worse for George III in the colonies. While the Wilkes affair occupied the king and Parliament, the royal governor of Massachusetts, Francis Bernard, took steps on his own to enforce the Townshend Acts. In June 1768, he ordered British officers to seize the *Liberty*, a ship that belonged to Boston's wealthiest merchant, John Hancock.

John Hancock resented and opposed the Townshend Acts.

King George III

Despite his great wealth, Hancock had become, with Samuel Adams, a leader of the anti-British colonists. Hancock had grown up with a deep hatred for the Navigation Acts and had smuggled goods into the colonies rather than pay import duties. Hundreds of angry longshoremen, the laborers who unloaded boats, showed their support for Hancock by burning a boat that belonged to the British customs officer, to protest the seizure of the *Liberty*.

With this action by the longshoremen, George III and Parliament reached the limit of their patience. They agreed that troops should be sent to Boston to enforce the Townshend Acts and to assert British authority. In October 1768, more than seven hundred red-coated British soldiers marched off troop ships into Boston. Before long, even more ships arrived, until a total of four thousand troops—two regiments in all—filled the city.

The redcoats needed housing, but anyone who offered to shelter them risked punishment from the Sons of Liberty. As a result, the troops were forced to camp on Boston Common. The army's presence only encouraged support for the efforts of Adams, Hancock, and others. The redcoats took over the marketplace at Fanueil Hall and, in an attempt to bully the colonists, aimed cannons at the statehouse, where the Massachusetts legislature met. The colonists, however, refused to be intimidated. Townspeople harassed the British troops. Youngsters tossed eggs and insults at them.

Ships carrying thousands of British soldiers docked at Boston in October 1768. Colonists resisted this attempt to implement British authority with harassment.

Adams started a propaganda campaign in the summer of 1768—one that was more extreme than the one he organized to protest the Stamp Act. This time, instead of reasoned essays, he planted exaggerated news stories that accused the British soldiers of beating citizens and worse. Adams's stories were exaggerated to the point that they would have been called libelous in Great Britain. Still, Bernard was recalled to answer charges that the redcoats had abused Boston residents.

## Lord North and the Boston Massacre

In 1770, George III celebrated ten years on the throne. He was in some ways a contradiction. On the one hand, he was a proud man who felt he had been given a divine right to rule the empire. On the other hand, he still suffered from a lack of self-confidence that stemmed from his childhood learning difficulties. In addition, the sickness that came and went had begun to affect his moods and made him unpredictable.

These personal difficulties were compounded by an instability in his appointment of prime ministers. In the first decade of his reign, George III had appointed seven prime ministers. These frequent changes had prevented the king from establishing a working relationship with Parliament.

The king's relationship with Parliament improved in 1770 when Lord Frederick North accepted the position of prime minister. North, at age thirty-eight, had known George III since childhood, and the king was comfortable with a man only slightly older than himself. In addition, North had served under several prime ministers during the king's first decade and was well aware of the mistakes each had made.

North immediately became one of the most popular prime ministers to hold the position. He was good-natured and a witty public speaker who understood the give-and-take that was necessary for

Lord Frederick North

success in politics. He did not belong to any political party and was thus able to attract various groups to support his views. Although North was a member of the House of Lords, his personality and experience helped him get along with even the most antiroyal members of the House of Commons. Unlike his predecessors, North was also an effective communicator between the king and Parliament. In fact, because of North's skills and his close friendship with the king, in the minds of colonists, George III became closely linked with Parliament's actions.

Even as relations between King George III and Parliament were improving, the king's relationship with his American colonists was deteriorating. The first incident under North's term that inflamed colonists took place in Boston in 1770. The British soldiers stationed there were paid so poorly that they often took part-time jobs when off duty. This practice meant that some American laborers lost work to the already unpopular soldiers. Indignant colonial workers taunted the soldiers, threw stones at them, and ganged up on them. The soldiers, even though they had been ordered to avoid violence as much as possible, often shoved and beat the colonists in return.

Tensions reached a breaking point on the night of March 5, when a crowd of men and boys began throwing rocks and snowballs at a British guard. When the guard called for help, his captain arrived with armed soldiers. Tempers were short. The colonists were still angry about the recent death of a young boy at the hands of a Loyalist merchant as well as the fact that redcoats were taking their jobs. On the other side, British troops were still angry from a beating suffered by one of their men at the hands of a band of colonists.

Soon a large group of colonists pressed closely against the smaller squad of redcoats. An officer may have yelled, "Do not *fire*!" In the noise, the soldiers claimed to have heard only *"fire!"*—and they started to shoot. Eleven Bostonians were hit by gunfire, and five died of their wounds.

The next morning, outraged colonists voted to send a delegation to the statehouse to demand the withdrawal of the troops. At the statehouse, royal governor Thomas Hutchinson said he did not have the authority to do any more than remove the regiment that was responsible.

Adams, who led the delegation, kept the colonists' outrage at a fever pitch. He called the killings "bloody butchery." He had his friend, the silver-smith and engraver Paul Revere, engrave a drawing that showed British soldiers firing point-blank at the crowd—a distortion of what actually happened. Hutchinson soon realized that he could not stand against the sentiments of an entire city. He agreed to remove both regiments, and within days, the redcoats marched back down to the wharves to board ships bound for Great Britain.

By coincidence, Parliament had repealed the Townshend Acts on the day of the bloody episode that became known as the Boston Massacre. The only tax that remained was the one levied on tea. Bostonians considered themselves victorious, and many hoped to put the unpleasant events of the preceding years behind them. Many pledged renewed loyalty to George III.

At this point, the idea of an independent nation without a king was beyond the imagination of many colonists. After all, no one at that time had known anything but rule by a monarch. Men such as Revere and Adams fell out "out of fashion," as Adams told his daughter. In late 1770, the boycott of British goods ended. Still, few protest leaders or members of the Sons of Liberty trusted the British. They decided that even in peaceful times, they had to remain informed of events in other colonies.

★

In 1771, Benjamin Franklin began to write his autobiography.

★

In 1772, colonists formed what they called Committees of Correspondence in Boston to communicate with other towns in Massachusetts. Eventually almost every colony had a committee to exchange information with other colonies about British actions in America. This established a communication network throughout the colonies, in case resistance was again required.

Meanwhile, across the Atlantic, the king and the British government faced another challenge from Wilkes, who had been released from prison in 1770. Wilkes sought revenge in the form of once again running for public office. Banned from running for Parliament, Wilkes ran for sheriff in

London. He was so popular that a group of Londoners organized a club to support him financially and speak on his behalf. Among those who joined the group was a customs official named Thomas Paine, who had earlier caused some turmoil in London by writing letters to Parliament in which he demanded higher wages for customs officers. With the support of Paine and many others, Wilkes was easily elected. He also began still another antigovernment publishing campaign.

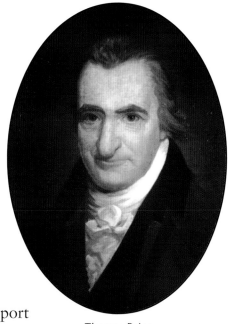

Thomas Paine

In 1771, the House of Commons had prevented several London newspapers from publishing reports of debates that occurred during its sessions. Wilkes decided to attempt to print the reports himself, and the government responded by arresting the men he had paid to print them. Wilkes led a large crowd to the House of Commons to protest the arrests. In response, North ordered the release of the printers. The government also ceased its attempts to prevent the publication of session reports.

Wilkes became so popular that he was elected mayor of London. He continued to be a presence on the political scene, but for the king and Great Britain, the real concern would soon be the American colonies.

# Chapter 4

## THE ROAD TO REBELLION

**D**espite the relative calm in relations between Great Britain and the American colonies, Governor Hutchinson was concerned about the activities of the Committees of Correspondence. In 1772, he wrote several letters to Lord North in which he asked for tougher policies against the colonies and requested that troops once again be sent to America. Although the letters were supposed to remain secret, they appeared in the *Boston Gazette* in 1773. Many colonists were outraged by the letters. Those who had been content to accept the tax on tea began to believe that it was only a matter of time before the hated redcoats returned.

OPPOSITE: Colonists disguised themselves as Native Americans at the Boston Tea Party, one of many acts of rebellion against the Crown.

Governor Thomas
Hutchinson

In fact, the Parliament and the king were less concerned with the American colonies than they were with British activities in another colony, India. A large British enterprise, the East India Company, had taken practical control of India for trade purposes. Furthermore, to protect its interests, the company had brought a private army to the colony.

George III and North did not like the idea of a private company and fighting force acting on behalf of the British government. In response, in 1773 North convinced Parliament to pass the Regulating Act for India, which placed government control over territory occupied by the East India Company. This was not an easy task for North and the king because many of the company's wealthiest backers were members of Parliament.

North and George III soon came up with a way to smooth over the political ill will that their act had caused. The East India Company, as it happened, was facing serious financial problems. It owed more than four hundred thousand pounds to the Bank of England and to the British government.

At the same time, the company had 15 million pounds of tea sitting in British warehouses, with more on the way from India. The company was oversupplied with tea because Americans, in protest of the tax that had been imposed in 1768, refused to buy it.

Officials of the East India Company asked North to repeal the tax on tea so that colonists would buy it, but simply as a matter of principle, George III refused to lift the tax. His concern was that to do so would be taken as a sign of weakness by the colonists. Instead, he and North submitted the Tea Act to Parliament. The Tea Act taxed the tea in India, but then allowed the company to ship it

This engraving depicts a meeting of the New York Sons of Liberty concerning the new Tea Act in the colonies.

directly to America. This meant that the company avoided having to pay another tax in British ports before reexporting it to the colonies. The net effect was to make the East India Company's tea cheaper than the smuggled tea the colonists were mostly drinking at the time. Finally, the Tea Act gave the East India Company sole rights to tea sales in the American colonies through any merchants they chose.

In the American colonies, the passage of the Tea Act drove merchants who had been selling smuggled tea out of business. In the eyes of the colonists, North and the king had forced the tea of Great Britain's largest company down their throats. Even worse, many colonists saw the tax break given to the East India Company as another example of favoritism to the wealthy, many said.

## Boston Tea Party

In the end, what George III and North believed was a convenient way to solve a problem caused them even greater problems. With the passage of the Tea Act, colonists mounted a campaign throughout the colonies to boycott tea. The boycott was so effective that sales of tea dropped by more than two-thirds. The government realized that it could not allow the boycott to continue, or the East India Company would go bankrupt—an economic disaster that would cripple the nation. George III and North, working through Parliament, decided to force the issue.

In November, three vessels loaded with tea were sent to Boston, protected by armed ships. In response, the Sons of Liberty told Governor Hutchinson that they would not let the ships unload their cargo. The governor refused to send the ships back. Adams, who had been a forgotten man over the prior three years, was once again ready to channel the resulting outrage among colonists into action.

Finally, on December 16, 1773, more than five thousand angry people assembled in the Old South Meeting House to protest the presence of British ships in Boston Harbor. At the meetinghouse, Adams stood up and declared, "This meeting can do nothing more to save the country!" At those words, nearly one hundred men painted their faces with coal dust and put feathers in their hair to disguise themselves as Indians. They brandished hatchets and shouted "T[ea] is for tyranny!" as they paraded to Griffin's Wharf.

In three groups, the men rowed out to the ships. Weapons raised, the raiders demanded the cargo hatch keys from the captains and broke into the holds. One by one, they smashed open crates of tea, 342 in all, and dumped them into the water. Word of what came to be called the Boston Tea Party soon spread to the other colonies. New York and Maryland patriots followed with similar actions, and in early 1774, a shipment of tea was destroyed in the southern port of Charleston, South Carolina.

★

In 1773, General Charles Cornwallis was the vice treasurer ot Ireland and was stationed in the Irish city of Cork.

★

59

## Intolerable Laws

Before the Boston Tea Party, major protests by colonists had caused Parliament to back away from its tax laws. This time, however, the colonists' actions drew a swift and tough response from Great Britain. Lord North and an enraged George III firmly believed that they had a moral right to expect the Americans to obey them just as their subjects in Great Britain did.

Because of slow communications, the news of tea revolts in other colonies did not reach London until after the news of events in Boston. As a result, the king and Parliament were under the impression that the rebellion was confined to Massachusetts. To punish that colony, British lawmakers, in a series of laws the colonists called the Intolerable Acts, closed the port of Boston. The acts banned Massachusetts towns from holding meetings, even those meant to settle local matters. Massachusetts officials accused of crimes had to be tried in England. Finally, a Quartering Act forced Boston residents to house and feed British troops sent there.

North also replaced Hutchinson as governor with General Thomas Gage, a military leader who had fought in the French and Indian War. Parliament prepared to send five thousand troops to Boston to support him. Tensions increased when Gage arrived in mid-May, with troops close behind. Once again there were dangerous clashes in the streets.

On December 16, 1773, angry colonists dumped 342 crates of tea into Boston Harbor (pictured). Patriots in other colonies soon followed the Bostonians' example.

In May 1774, the Boston Committee of Correspondence sent letters to the other colonies to report that the port would be closed. Colonial committees offered to aid Massachusetts by opening their ports to Boston-bound ships and sending supplies overland to the beleaguered city.

## The First Continental Congress

As a result of the British actions against Boston, committees in other colonies agreed to hold a meeting to determine whether they should take unified steps against the Crown. On June 17, 1774, Adams made a secret motion in the Massachusetts House to send five delegates to the colonywide Continental Congress in Philadelphia. Adams, his cousin John Adams, Hancock, and two other men were selected.

At the first session of the Continental Congress, which opened on September 5, 1774, representatives from twelve of the thirteen colonies filled Carpenter's Hall. On September 17, the Massachusetts delegation introduced what were called the Suffolk Resolves.

This document described the situation in their colony and called for a boycott of British goods in response. When the document was read, the hall burst into cheers, and many delegates vowed to support Massachusetts.

In London, as news of the congressional meeting reached George III, he realized the extent of resistance to Britain's rule in America. The king saw, for the first time, the possibility that armed conflict might occur. In September 1774, he wrote in his diary: "The colonies must either submit or triumph. I do not wish to come to severer measures, but we must not retreat."

The First Continental Congress met at Carpenter's Hall (pictured) in Philadelphia.

King George III

At the congressional meeting, however, few delegates, no matter how dissatisfied they were with the policies of the British government, were ready to consider the prospect of war against the Crown. For some, even the Suffolk Resolves were too radical. One delegate said they "contained a complete declaration of war against Great Britain."

As the session continued, Congress agreed to send a formal appeal to the king to moderate his policies. The new appeal, at least in the view of the more radical delegates, understated the colonists' indignation. They were infuriated by what they considered a weak appeal to George III's "wisdom, goodness, and concern for his people's welfare."

Before the Congress adjourned, the representatives agreed that the colonies should boycott incoming British goods and halt the export of American products to Great Britain. The delegates also agreed to arm and drill volunteer military units called militias in case they were needed to fight British troops. Plans were made to assemble again the following spring in Philadelphia.

In London, the king learned of the boycott and became even more convinced that the only answer was force. He wrote in his diary on November 18, 1774: "Blows must decide whether they are to be subject to this country or independent."

As 1775 began, a buildup toward war became evident in and around Boston. Members of the patriot militia, calling themselves minutemen because they could theoretically be assembled on a minute's notice, drilled in towns around Boston. Meanwhile, additional British troops poured into the city. Refugees fled Boston, which suffered a food shortage caused by the trade embargo. Redcoats took over homes and openly harassed any citizens who expressed anti-British sentiments.

Throughout late winter and into early spring of 1775, each side cautiously noted the other's activities. Whenever patriots held meetings in the city, soldiers watched them and waited for a chance to arrest Adams and Hancock, should they appear. On the patriot side, groups of colonists walked the streets of Boston in pairs, taking note of the movements of British soldiers.

General Thomas Gage planned to crush the American revolt.

On April 14, orders arrived for Gage, authorizing him to act immediately against "proceedings that amount to actual revolt." He was ordered to seize the leaders of the colonial protests—Adams and Hancock. In addition, Gage was ordered to take all weapons and military supplies away from the rebels.

The orders, which had been issued in January, signaled that

Parliament—and, by association, George III—had run out of patience with its American subjects. William, the earl of Dartmouth, a member of the House of Lords, spoke for Parliament and the king when he stated, "It is the opinion of the King's servants, in which His Majesty concurs, that the first and essential step to be taken towards reestablishing Government, would be to arrest and imprison the principal actors and abettors of the Provincial Congress whose proceedings appear... to be acts of treason."

George III and Parliament had reason to believe that it would be a simple matter to crush a rebellion in the American colonies. British troops had, after all, recently ended revolts in other parts of the British Empire, such as Ireland, Scotland, and India. Many of the experienced soldiers stationed in Boston had also served in Ireland and Scotland and knew how to deal with rebels. Others had experience keeping the peace and stopping riots that had resulted from the controversy surrounding Wilkes's activities.

In response to Parliament's orders, Gage drew up plans to march to Concord and capture the supplies that were believed to be stored there. Gage also hoped to capture Hancock and Adams. Spies had reported that the two men had left Boston to attend a meeting and were probably somewhere in Lexington, located between Boston and Concord.

In fact, the two men were in Lexington. Throughout those days, as they had for months,

On April 19, 1775, minutemen faced British soldiers on Lexington Green, Massachusetts. That exchange of fire began the American Revolution.

Boston colonists kept a close eye on British movement. In early April, news spread among them that the British planned to march out of Boston to capture Adams and Hancock, and then continue to Concord to seize the militia's powder and weapons. Immediately, a system of signals was established to alert the Sons of Liberty in nearby towns when the redcoats began their operation.

At dawn on April 19, 1775, the first shots of the American Revolution were fired on Lexington Green, where seven hundred British soldiers confronted about seventy minutemen. The British troops quickly dispersed the minutemen and then marched on to Concord. There they were met by minutemen who had come by the hundreds from nearby towns to resist the redcoats.

By the afternoon of that unusually warm spring day, the British had been driven out of Concord and were in full retreat back to the safety of Boston. After they witnessed the historic battle, Adams and Hancock began the long journey south to Philadelphia to help create a new government. It would be several months before word of the historic events reached Parliament and George III across the Atlantic.

# Chapter 5

## THE UNCERTAIN YEAR

As news of the Battle of Lexington and Concord reached Great Britain, George III and North found widespread support for their decision to fight the rebellious colonists. That support came from wealthy landowners, university professors, religious leaders, and many working-class British subjects. Even Wilkes, the mayor of London, supported British actions in Massachusetts. In a letter in 1775, North wrote: "The violent measures towards America are fairly adopted and countenanced by a majority of all individuals of all ranks, professions or occupations in this country."

OPPOSITE: This painting depicts the Continental Congress's appointment of George Washington as commanding general of their newly created army.

69

Although supportive of war, many delegates of the Second Continental Congress (pictured) still felt loyal to George III.

In the colonies, the Continental Congress met for the second time in May 1775. News of the battles the month before had spread quickly, carried by the messengers of the Committees of Correspondence. The colonists were now aware that the British would not hesitate to use warfare to enforce their domination of America.

The task of the Second Continental Congress was to consider what John Adams called "the dangerous and critical situation" in the colonies. The incidents at Lexington and Concord had convinced most delegates that war was necessary, but they disagreed on what they hoped to accomplish by going to war. While a growing number of delegates were ready to fight for complete independence, many hoped to reconcile their differences and remain loyal to George III and Britain.

By that time, Gage had declared martial law in Boston—all laws would be enforced by the military, instead of the city's judicial system. Colonists were ordered to lay down their arms or be considered traitors. More soldiers arrived from Great Britain, as did two more generals, John Burgoyne and William Howe.

King George III

Boston patriots sought aid from the Continental Congress, and the delegates issued requests for companies of riflemen to march to Massachusetts from the other colonies. On June 14, the delegates created an official Continental army "for the defense of American Liberty." John Adams nominated Washington as the commanding general, and Congress approved the nomination.

Even Washington was uncertain that complete independence from Great Britain was wise, although he was ready to use armed force to protect the colonists' rights if that became necessary. Washington arrived in Boston shortly after the Battle of Bunker Hill, and he saw in the violence of that clash further proof that the colonists would soon be in an all-out conflict with the most powerful military in the world.

When news of the British losses at Bunker Hill reached London in early July 1775, North realized that events in the colonies were rapidly heading toward all-out war. He felt that he was unqualified to fulfill the many responsibilities that would result from such a turn of events. North offered his resignation to George III, but the king refused to accept it. He had no one else to take the position, and his bond with North was something that he could not replace.

★

In the spring of 1775, Scottish immigrant John Paul Jones left Virginia for Philadelphia to seek a commission in the newly formed Continental navy.

★

What made North's position especially difficult was that he was responsible for finding a way to pay for the war. It was his job to buy the equipment, supplies, and food the army needed. He also had to

71

make arrangements for transporting these goods to the troops. This enormous amount of material had to be assembled in English ports and shipped to the colonies. With the nation still in debt, the prime minister had to accomplish the task as economically as possible.

As prime minister, North, in consultation with George III, was also responsible for choosing the secretary to America, who would take on the responsibility for determining the strategy of the war and assigning the generals who would carry out that strategy. The earl of Dartmouth had resigned from the position in 1775 shortly after the Battle of Lexington and Concord. North wasted little time in naming George Germain, the lord of Sackville, to this position. Germain had been an officer in the Seven Years' War and had expressed strong dislike of the colonists' refusal to pay taxes for their defense. He took his post determined to force the colonies to submit to the rule of George III and Parliament. He began by telling Parliament that a peace commission to search for a possible compromise with colonial leaders was out of the question. There was to be no compromise, Germain insisted.

## Two Petitions by Congress

Despite the events in Boston, the Continental Congress remained far from unanimous in its attitude toward Great Britain. This discord came at a time when members of Congress faced critical issues on which they had to reach some agreement.

The colonies had no central government and no model to follow for such a government. There was little gunpowder or artillery and few factories to manufacture either item. There was national currency and no system for raising money to support a military. The colonies had many merchant sailors but no warships. The army consisted of untrained, inexperienced militias. Perhaps the most serious problem was that in every colony—especially in the south—there were many men and women who were not interested in independence and remained loyal to Great Britain.

Congress fiercely debated over the Olive Branch Petition (pictured), which sought compromise over independence.

In late June, Congress issued a new petition to George III that outlined American grievances, but also humbly sought compromise. The petition was controversial, since many delegates who favored independence hated the document. The debate was so bitter that those who sought compromise threatened to break away from the New England colonies that wanted independence to make a separate agreement with the king. New England delegates compared the petition to holding a sword in one hand and an olive branch (a symbol of peace) in the other—that, in fact, became the name of the document: the Olive Branch Petition. After approval

On June 15, 1775,
George Washington
was named commander
in chief of the
Continental army.

of the petition, two delegates sailed to
London to personally deliver it to George III.

The dissatisfaction with the Olive Branch
Petition among some members of Congress
was so deep, however, that even as the
two delegates set off, another petition was
written and approved. This petition, Declaration of
the Causes and Necessity of Taking Up Arms, was
distributed in the colonies and printed in newspapers
in Europe. In it, the world heard the defiance of the
delegates who called the British enemies and
reaffirmed their determination:

> Our cause is just. . . . Our internal resources
> are great, and . . . foreign assistance is undoubt-
> edly attainable. . . . With hearts fortified . . . we
> most solemnly . . . declare that . . . the arms we
> have been compelled by our enemies to assume,
> we will, in defiance of, employ for the preser-
> vation of our liberties; being with one mind
> resolved to die freemen rather than to live slaves.

In Parliament, North responded to the Olive
Branch Petition with an offer. Great Britain would
repeal taxes used to pay for royal appointees
and troops in the colonies, he said, but it would
keep the right to levy taxes to regulate colonial
commerce. Despite the compromise, however,
North also flatly refused to allow the delegates
an audience with George III. Thus, they could not
present the king with the "olive branch," as many

of the delegates to the Continental Congress desired. They returned to America and conveyed North's offer to Congress.

Once again, Congress was divided. Those delegates unwilling to fully break from Great Britain wanted to accept North's offer. Adams and other independence-minded delegates saw North's plan as an attempt to divide Americans. Adams was angered further when North sent a letter in which

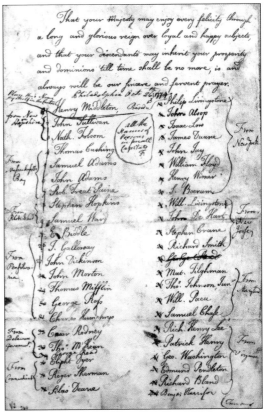

While many members of Congress signed the Olive Branch Petition, others drafted a very different petition that called for war.

he threatened to use the "whole force of the Kingdom . . . to reduce [conquer] the rebellious . . . Colonies" if they did not accept the proposal.

George III also felt that the colonists were rebelling at their own risk. His proclamation in late summer 1775 was a stern warning to those who he said were being led by those with "traitorous designs." In a speech to Parliament in October 1775, he said: "It is now become the part of wisdom . . . to put a speedy end to these disorders by the most decisive exertions."

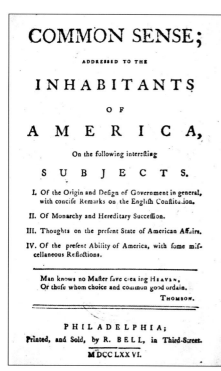

Common Sense, a pamphlet written by Thomas Paine, outlined reasons for the colonies to break away from Great Britain.

## Common Sense

As 1776 arrived, the colonists were certain that George III and Parliament meant to impose their will by military force. At the same time, many colonists and delegates were still not completely convinced that the colonies should split completely with Great Britain. The task of convincing the colonists that independence was necessary was taken on by a man who had arrived in Philadelphia less than a year earlier. His name was Thomas Paine, the same individual who a few years earlier had been a supporter of Wilkes.

In January 1776, Paine published a pamphlet in which he laid out the reasons why the colonies should break away from Great Britain. Paine did not mince words in the pamphlet, which he titled *Common Sense*. He knew that he was speaking boldly, but the cause that he supported was one that extended beyond the colonies. "The cause of America is in a great measure the cause of all mankind," he wrote in the introduction.

Paine began *Common Sense* by dealing with the subject of government, which he called "a necessary

King George III

evil." He described an ideal government as one that arose from the people, then contrasted this ideal government with monarchy, a form of government that he called "exceedingly ridiculous."

Paine continued by taking direct aim at George III in an effort to provide the colonists with an object on which to focus their anger. A king is a contradiction, said Paine, because the "state of a king shuts him from the world, yet the business of a king requires him to know it thoroughly." Paine said kings such as George III are "absurd and useless." What made monarchy worse, Paine went on, was the practice of succession—rulers who passed their throne on to their children. "Monarchy and succession have laid . . . the world in blood and ashes," he wrote.

Paine then addressed the main point of his pamphlet, his reason why the colonies should separate from Great Britain. Though many colonists regarded it as the mother country, he said, Great Britain had failed in that role, since a true parent would protect its offspring. Instead, Great Britain had persecuted the colonists "with the cruelty of a monster." He wrote, 'Shame upon her conduct. Even brutes do not devour their young; nor savages make war upon their families."

The pamphlet found an immediate audience. At a time when every country in the world was ruled by a monarch, Paine's words were astonishing to those who read them. Its first printing sold out in two weeks. In a few months, more than 150,000 copies had been sold. Farmers, tradesmen, women, soldiers, and politicians read it. The many colonists who could not read had others read it aloud to them.

Paine's tone of urgency inflamed the hearts of the patriots. People began to understand that they could progress economically only through independence, which would allow the money they paid in taxes to be used to their overall benefit. If they waited, British tyranny would increase; American taxes would go to support tyrants rather than public good.

Soldiers gathered in Boston in the winter of 1776 passed around copies of *Common Sense*, while Washington struggled to shape a new Continental army. Many soldiers still were not fully sure why they should agree to fight. Washington noted that as they read Paine's pamphlet aloud around their campfires, it began "working a wonderful change in the minds of many men."

A change also occurred across the Atlantic after Paine's pamphlet arrived there. The idea that a king and a government

Paine's *Common Sense* inspired colonists to fight British tyranny.

King George III

In the spring of 1776, British ships assembled in New York harbor in an effort to control the colonies.

should pay attention to public opinion was an entirely new concept. Yet within months after *Common Sense* reached Great Britain, a large number of other works were published that argued in favor of a more democratic government. These works arose at a time when Great Britain was shifting from being an agricultural society to an industrial one. Workers, inspired by Paine's work and other writings, began to agitate for a voice in government, much as the colonists had been doing. Groups such as the Society for the Supporters of a Bill of Rights formed and began to hold public meetings in which they pushed for a British constitution that would give rights to common people.

As concerned as North and George III were about rising civil unrest at home, their main attention was focused on bringing the colonies under control. In February, Parliament issued a prohibition on trade with the colonies and began a blockade of the entire coastline from Boston to Charleston, South Carolina. Germain ordered a large armada of ships and soldiers to assemble in New York harbor in the spring of 1776.

79

# Chapter 6

## REVOLUTION
## AND DEFEAT

**B**y the spring of 1776, the members of Congress had begun to receive urgent instructions from their home legislatures to move toward self-rule. On June 7, 1776, Henry Lee of Virginia made a formal motion to declare America a union of independent states. The delegates selected a committee including thirty-three-year-old Thomas Jefferson of Virginia, to prepare the official declaration.

OPPOSITE: This painting depicts the surrender of Charles Cornwallis at Yorktown, Virginia. The British surrender on October 18, 1781, effectively ended the war in America.

Public readings of the Declaration of Independence recharged the colonists as they prepared for battle with the British.

On July 4, John Hancock, the president of the Congress, affixed his bold signature to the document called the Declaration of Independence. He wrote in such a large hand, he said, so George III "can read my name without spectacles and may double his reward on my head!" The declaration was circulated throughout the colonies and read aloud to cheering crowds from statehouse steps and balconies.

At Washington's order, on July 9 patriot troops assembled on New York Island (today known as Manhattan). The commander read the document publicly to his troops, who reacted with a joyous cheer. In one city square, several soldiers threw a rope around a huge metal statue of George III and pulled it over. Men jeered the fallen image of the

King George III

British king and boasted about driving the redcoats back across the Atlantic. The metal was taken away to be melted into musket balls.

## Early British Success

Once the celebrations ended, the patriots quickly realized that they faced an almost impossible challenge. The British army had more than thirty thousand professional soldiers in New York alone. Great Britain also had the largest and most powerful navy in the world. British ships had blockaded the coast from Massachusetts to South Carolina to prevent merchant ships from entering or leaving the colonies. The American navy, by contrast, consisted of about twenty-five merchant ships that had been refitted with cannons—no match for the British warships.

The imbalance of power worked to the British advantage in the initial years of the war. No sooner had the patriots pulled down the statue of George III in New York, than they were completely defeated in the Battle of Long Island in August 1776. By the end of 1776, Washington and his ragged forces were in retreat across New Jersey toward Philadelphia.

★

In August 1776, delegates in Philadelphia signed the formal parchment copy of the Declaration of Independence.

★

Washington felt that the war's end was near. British troops had taken control of Long Island, New York City, Staten Island, and most of New Jersey. They seemed ready to attack Pennsylvania. Early in December, the British navy took over

83

The British army was a powerful force but did not have strong leadership. Cornwallis (pictured with sword) and many other British officers lacked proper military training.

Newport, Rhode Island, and there set up a naval station where military supplies could be off-loaded.

Washington commanded two victories at Trenton and Princeton as the winter of 1777 arrived, bringing some hope to Americans. Those victories, however, meant more for patriot morale that they did for the colonists' strategic position. By late summer 1777, British forces were near Philadelphia, and the Continental Congress had fled the city.

Although the British army was the most powerful in the world, it did have weaknesses that kept it from achieving total victory even when it held an advantage. One weakness was its leadership. Great Britain had no military academy to train men for the job of commanding others. Most men became officers by purchasing commissions or by being appointed, thanks to influential friends. Such a system meant that officers came from the richest classes—the landowners and the aristocracy. Men who wanted to become officers had only to pay a great deal of money to receive commissions from the king—talent had little to do with the choice of military leaders.

British officers often viewed their service as a chance to gain personal fame at home, and they often cared little about their military responsibilities. They had little concept of what fighting a war involved. General John Burgoyne, for example, was called "Gentleman Johnny" by his troops because he needed sixty wagons to carry all of his luggage—including fine china—when on a march. Yet the entire force he commanded had only forty wagons for its supplies.

The lack of military experience affected officers at critical times. William Howe, for example, was so confident of victory on Long Island that he stopped his attack to allow troops to eat. When a sudden rainstorm blew in, the British troops were stuck in a position that allowed Washington's army time to escape. Charles Cornwallis, who commanded British forces in the South, marched his army into what turned out to be an indefensible position at Yorktown in 1781.

As the war dragged on, another weakness became apparent. British troops were more accustomed to subduing unarmed peasants, not determined rebels. Many British men refused to volunteer to fight in the American Revolution, because the Americans

85

The thick, woolen uniforms of the British army, worn by modern-day reenactors in this photo, caused some redcoats to die of heat exhaustion.

fought so fiercely. As the enlistments declined, the army tried to fill out the ranks first with convicts who were offered the chance to earn their freedom if they served. Even this approach failed to fill the ranks, so the British army took any man between the ages of sixteen and fifty-five who stood at least five feet, three inches tall. There were still not enough men for the British army, so the king decided to hire mercenaries—called Hessians—from several German states to meet his military needs.

Whatever their background, troops fighting on the British side found themselves poorly prepared to wage war in the vast expanses of the American colonies. At the same time, their supplies and weapons were not appropriate for the type of war they were required to fight. For example, British uniforms were made of wool. This fabric was warm in the winter, but armies did not fight during the coldest months, when rain turned roads to quagmires or snow blocked them altogether. In warm weather, when armies could fight, wool was extremely uncomfortable, especially in the humidity of the middle and southern colonies.

Foot soldiers were required to march long distances in full uniform carrying large packs that contained a change of clothes, food, and water. They usually marched into battle with sixty pounds of equipment on their backs. Heat exhaustion was a common cause of death for redcoats during the war.

British soldiers were also burdened with weapons that were ineffective. Each man carried a firearm called the Brown Bess, which was a smoothbore flintlock almost five feet long. A complicated weapon to operate, the Brown Bess fired a one-ounce musket ball and was only accurate up to about fifty yards. A commanding officer then had to give more than thirty separate orders to reload after each volley. The gun could not be fired in wet weather, because rain or snow would soak the powder in the priming pan.

Almost one-third of the American soldiers had no shoes, and most had no blankets or warm clothing.

The Brown Bess, however, was very effective in one regard: It could be mounted with a bayonet—a two-foot-long, razor-sharp knife. Massed charges of men armed in this way were fearsome, and such charges—or even the threat of one—accounted for the early British successes in many battles and skirmishes. Colonial troops ran in terror from the bayonet charges in the first years of the war.

87

## France Becomes an Ally

In spite of the disadvantages they faced, British forces seemed to have the Americans on the defensive. Then, in late October came news of an important American victory. Patriot forces had defeated British troops commanded by Burgoyne at Saratoga, New York, giving the colonials control of the Hudson River and New England. This key American victory was taken as evidence that the rebels could win and convinced France to enter the war on the side of the rebels.

When news of the French decision to enter the war reached London, North, who was rapidly losing public support, once again tried to resign. Once again, George III refused to allow it. North and the king realized that an expanded war with France would place a serious strain on the weak British economy, so North sought George III's permission

The defeat of General John Burgoyne, pictured here as he surrenders his sword, convinced the French to join patriot forces.

to make peace with the colonies. He convinced the king to support a plan in Parliament that would repeal all laws passed since 1763 and allow the colonies a limited amount of self-rule.

The king agreed, and North created the Carlisle Commission, which offered the colonists all that they had been demanding— except independence. A group of peace commissioners sailed to America in 1778 to begin negotiations. The offer from North's commission arrived after the French had signed an official treaty alliance with America, however, and the Continental Congress refused to consider the British offer of compromise.

★

Benjamin Franklin and John Adams were ministers to France in 1778.

★

## Final Years

For much of 1778 and 1779, the two opposing armies in the Northeast remained in a stalemate. British forces were safe in heavily fortified New York City, and most of the American troops were encamped in the area around the city. Washington remained frustrated in his attempts to solve the problems that had plagued him throughout the war—short terms of enlistment, lack of pay for his troops, and shortages of supplies. For example, his army in the East spent much of 1779 in camp because of a shortage of shoes.

The British also faced problems that kept them from achieving the upper hand in the war. The main difficulty stemmed from the fact that their army was three thousand miles from home.

89

French forces successfully attacked many British transport ships. Although such losses hurt Britain's economy, George III refused to give up the colonies.

Troops, horses, guns, and ammunition had to be transported across the Atlantic in slow-sailing ships. Once France entered the war, British transport ships came increasingly under attack from French naval vessels. Hundreds of transport ships were seized or sunk, which severely hurt the already weak British economy.

By 1779, many members of Parliament had become sick of the war's drain on the British economy. Dissatisfaction had been rising in Great Britain among working classes, and it now spread to wealthier members of society, the landholders, as North sought to offset some of the war's expenses by raising property taxes. In response, landholders complained bitterly that they were not only losing money, they were losing the war. In protest, they formed the County Association to encourage antiroyal and antiwar candidates to run for local and national office. Public sentiment about the war, which had supported George III in 1775, began to turn strongly in support of independence for the colonies.

Despite the growing antiwar sentiment among his subjects, George III refused to agree to a withdrawal of troops. He agreed that the war was economically harmful, but, he argued, the war was necessary for the empire to remain powerful. If a rebellion succeeded in America, the king reasoned, similar revolts might again arise in Ireland, India, or other important colonies.

Despite the conflicts in London over the war, Germain believed the army could simply outlast the Americans in the North and then turn their attention to the South, where, he believed, there was a stronger loyalist sentiment. In addition, the wealthy southern colonies, with their tobacco and cotton crops, had always been more economically attractive to the British. Lord North and the king eagerly agreed to this strategy in hopes that its success would satisfy critics in Great Britain by convincing them that retaining control over the South would ease their tax burden.

In 1777, British infantry attacked sleeping American soldiers in the village of Paoli, Pennsylvania, killing fifty men and wounding hundreds.

In 1780, British forces under Cornwallis attacked Charleston, South Carolina, the largest city in the South. American regular troops and Patriot militia there held out for a month before they surrendered. British forces then continued

King George III

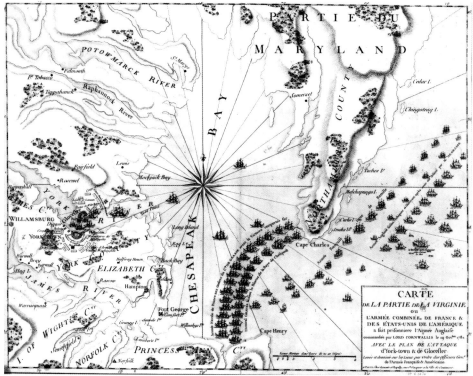

This French map shows the positions of American and French ships when they surrounded British troops encamped at Yorktown.

their march through the South for much of 1780. By the spring of 1781, they were in Virginia.

Around that time, French forces landed in Rhode Island and marched to join Washington's army in New York. In addition, a French fleet with thirty-five hundred troops and more than thirty huge cannons sailed into the Chesapeake Bay in Virginia in early September. Washington decided to lead a combined American and French force south to meet the French fleet. There they planned to jointly confront the British southern force that had camped at Yorktown, Virginia.

92

Cornwallis was expecting to receive weapons and reinforcements from New York; what he was not expecting was a fleet of French warships arriving at the same time as the combined French and American forces. While the Americans and French set off from New York, marching twenty-five to thirty miles a day, a French fleet blockaded the York River, cutting off the British escape route from Yorktown. Once Washington's forces arrived, the British were trapped and outnumbered. The Battle of Yorktown began in early October and was over within a few days. On October 18, 1781, the French lined one side of the Yorktown-Williamsburg Road and the Americans the other side as British and Hessian troops marched out of Yorktown to surrender.

The news of the combined American-French triumph reached Philadelphia on October 24. Across the colonies, Americans celebrated the victory. Word of the British surrender at Yorktown reached London one month later, on November 24, 1781. When North heard the news, he exclaimed, "Oh God, it's all over!" Though a formal peace treaty was not signed until two years later, the fighting that began on Lexington Green in Massachusetts had concluded in Yorktown, Virginia. On September 3, 1783, the peace treaty that ended the war was finally signed in Paris.

★

John Adams was a key member of the team that negotiated the formal peace treaty.

★

# Chapter 7

## FINAL YEARS

The end of the conflict in Great Britain's former colonies did little to end the king's domestic troubles. By the time the Treaty of Paris was signed, George III had been on the throne for twenty-two years. He was forty-five years old, and his reign had been one of almost constant crisis.

By 1783, North had so little support in Parliament that he resigned from his position as prime minister. His resignation came at a time when public support of the king was very low, and a number of political organizations were calling for reforms that would make the king little more than a figurehead.

OPPOSITE: In his final years, a blind George III completely succumbed to mental illness.

North was followed by three prime ministers, Lords Rockingham, Shelburne, and Bentinck, whose terms lasted less than a year each. None of the men had the skill to strengthen relations between the king and Parliament. By 1783, the king's relations with Parliament—especially the Whigs in the House of Commons—were so poor that he considered stepping down from the throne.

In 1784, however, a new prime minister took office at the age of twenty-four. He was William Pitt the Younger, the son of the man who had served George III in the 1760s. Few people expected the young Pitt to handle the heavy pressures of the job, but he remained in office until 1801. Pitt's first task was to address the nation's economic problems, which he did by increasing trade, revising tax policies, and cutting government spending. His investment ideas with tax funds helped bring down the national debt, and by the end of the 1780s, Pitt was considered the most brilliant economic mind ever to serve as prime minister.

William Pitt the Younger

## Mental Illness

Great Britain was also fortunate to have Pitt in office in the late 1780s because George III became ill again. The loss of the colonies and the political aftermath had been so stressful that the king suffered an attack of porphyria in 1788. The first indications of the attack were stiffness and pain in his arms and legs. Then, he complained that he was having difficulty seeing and hearing clearly. Even more disturbing for those around him, the king had a mental breakdown.

The mental breakdown resulted in the king talking constantly—sometimes shouting one word over and over—for hours at a time. Eventually, his speech became incoherent and he suffered hallucinations. He flew into senseless rages one moment, then sank into silent depression the next.

Doctors still had no idea exactly what was causing the king's symptoms. The treatments, based on the assumption that some sort of toxin or infection was responsible, did more harm than good. For example, physicians burned the king's forehead with hot irons in the belief that the blisters would "draw the poison out of his brain." When this failed, they kept the king in an unheated room during the winter in order to freeze whatever might be causing the disease.

As the king's psychotic episodes grew worse, his doctors restrained him in a straitjacket. When his rages became too loud, they gave him medicine to make him vomit the "fury" from his system. Again, such treatments were of no help.

97

Eventually, George III began to get better on his own, and within six months he was able to resume his royal duties. Once he regained his health, George III became extremely hardworking and read all documents put before him.

As the 1790s arrived, another revolution occurred, this time in France. The revolt pitted French nobility against the workers and peasants. People in Great Britain were divided about which side to support in the struggle. Both Pitt and George III, however, knew that the country had to remain neutral for economic reasons.

★

In 1798, Thomas Paine lived in Paris after his release from a French prison where he had been confined during that nation's revolution.

★

That neutrality ended in 1793, when the king of France, Louis XVI, was overthrown and executed. The antiroyal revolutionaries then declared war on Great Britain. For the next twenty years, the two nations engaged in battles that took place primarily at sea.

Both nations attempted to harm each other economically by interrupting trade relations. This French and British policy resulted in American merchant ships being seized on the high seas by warships from both countries. Relations between the United States and France reached a point close to war in 1798. Then, in 1807, in one of his final acts, George III signed the Orders in Council, a policy that asserted the right of the British navy to seize any trading vessels headed for French ports. British warships seized hundreds of American merchant ships over the following years. It was this act by George III that led directly to the War of 1812 between the United States and Great Britain.

In 1810, an attack of porphyria again manifested itself as mental illness, and George III sank further into insanity. In 1811, Parliament's Regency Council voted to allow George's son, the Prince of Wales, to assume the role of Prince Regent, which allowed him to assume the king's powers.

George III spent the last ten years of his life deaf, blind, lonely, and incoherent, wandering the halls of the royal castles in his nightshirt. When he died in 1820, he had been on the throne for sixty years.

Today, George III is remembered as having been an object of ridicule and anger among American patriots. To the colonists, he represented the one person who had total control over their lives. In truth, as the king of Great Britain, he had far less power than colonists realized. The decisions that brought about the American Revolution were made primarily by Parliament and the king's prime ministers. Yet even though the king and the colonies were separated by distance and understanding, their histories were closely linked. The path of each was determined by the actions of the other.

# Glossary

**activism**  organized political action to protest policy

**boycott**  an organized refusal to buy certain goods

**Continental Congress**  the first congress of united colonies

**Crown**  the royal British monarch and ministers

**Hessian**  a mercenary soldier from one of the states in Germany who fought for the king of England during the American Revolution

**House of Burgesses**  a legislative body representing boroughs or towns in Virginia

**Loyalist**  a person who supported the ruling government in Great Britain or the colonies

**militia**  a body of citizens called out to fight in emergencies

**Navigation Acts**  laws passed by the British Parliament in the late 1600s that controlled trade between England and the colonies

**Parliament**  the legislative division of English government, made up of the House of Commons and the House of Lords

**patriots**  colonists who supported and fought for independence from Great Britain

**porphyria**  a hereditary disease whose symptoms may include mental illness

100

**propaganda** materials sent out by members of a movement representing their views and principles

**radical** a person who holds extreme or contrary views

**redcoats** British soldiers, who wore red-jacketed uniforms

**repeal** to withdraw officially, as a law or an act

**Tory** the name given to the Loyalists in Great Britain and the colonies

**treason** a violation of allegiance to one's country

**tyranny** the abuse of power by a tyrant

**Whigs** antiroyal members of Parliament in Great Britain

# For More Information

**Books**

Jean Fritz, *Can't You Make Them Behave, King George?* New York: Coward McCann & Geoghegan, 1996.

Anne Gaines, *King George III: English Monarch.* Broomall, PA: Chelsea House, 2000.

Robert Green, *King George III.* Danbury, CT: Franklin Watts, 1997.

Allan Lloyd, *The King Who Lost America: A Portrait of the Life and Times of George III.* New York: Doubleday, 2002.

**Websites**
**British History**
(www.britannia.com)
Excellent overall reference on Great Britain's history.

**History of the Monarchy**
(www.royal.gov.uk)
Biographies of all British rulers from 1603.

**The American Revolution**
(www.theamericanrevolution.org)
Good all-around background on key events.

**PRO Virtual Museum**
(www.pro.gov.uk)
The online national archives of the United Kingdom.

# Index

103